U

Vanessa Dias-Carter

BookLeaf Publishing

Presentation by *BookLeaf Publishing*

Web: www.bookleafpub.com

E-mail: info@bookleafpub.com

ISBN: 978-93-95890-91-5

First edition 2022

DEDICATION

Lilian and Christiaan for reading every word, I have ever written, sometimes after being woken up in the middle of the night.

Mike, Sean, and Aedan, for loving me unconditionally.

ACKNOWLEDGEMENT

I could not have done this, if wasn't for Facebook ads and a late-night scroll through my feed, so thanks facebook for being always there looking through my google searches, but most importantly, I'm very thankful to my dear friend Sinéade that even during her holidays, took the task of checking my English and for editing some of the texts, if you find any mistakes, these will be the ones I edited myself.

PREFACE

I'm not a writer, a poet, or anything of sorts, I'm an absolute lover of words and how they can help you heal, understand yourself and laugh at the most unusual, ridiculous thoughts that come to your mind.

Writing

Writing is pouring out on the paper what overwhelms you inside and it is much more socially acceptable than running naked, screaming your head off.!

Dancing

I write like I dance; without following any set
steps, in an uncoordinated way.

I write like I dance;
with passion, emotion, and a degree of
clumsiness.

I write like I dance; for no one else but myself.

I write like I dance; letting the flow and the
rhythm take over me.

I write like I dance.
It might look, unkempt, unattractive even, look
closer though and you'll find beauty.

Reality

Everybody dreams of someone that will be 'the one'. The one person that you will laugh with, the one that listens to every boring opinion you have about every little detail of life, that ponders with you over endless life questions, that nods with vigorous enthusiasm at all your ifs and buts and future imaginings, that will be all attentive, in love, happy, easy-going, a dreamer.

Suddenly you find someone that seems to fit the bill perfectly. You start looking at the world a little smugly. "Look at you bunch of losers. All that you are looking for, will possibly never find, I have!! Can you hear me? I found it!! I found that someone that I will share the rest of my days with and not because I don't want to be homeless, nor because we have kids and divorce would be too complicated and messy or he is an abusive lunatic that is forcing me to stay in the relationship. No, none of those things. I will do it because I want to!! And I will love and cherish even his least charming inadequacies with patience and care. "Hey baby, have you seen my blue jumper I left on the kitchen table?"
"I don't know where your #&#@&#&# jumper is."

Unsettled

Sylvia opened her eyes at exactly 5:30. It happened every morning, but today something was wrong, or should I say more wrong than it had been in the past few years. She lay there as if paralysed. She didn't want to get up, as getting up meant having to live another day in a life that she could no longer envisage.

You would be forgiven for thinking that Sylvia had a bad life. After all, it all sounds quite depressing, but no, not at all, she had a life many would envy. She had a beautiful house near the beach with a beautiful garden, she worked with like-minded people that loved her and helped others like she always wanted. Her children adored her, her husband could not be more devoted, she had friends, many. She had freedom and the autonomy to pursue her favourite hobbies, or whatever her heart desired; she enjoyed her life.

I can see you scratching your head now and even cursing at her a little, maybe even asking how someone can be so ungrateful.

Well, Sylvia has what you could call the 'unsettled syndrome'. I know what you are thinking, this is not a 'condition'. Well, just because psychologists haven't come up with a name doesn't mean it is not real. Anyway, Sylvia is one of those people who is destined to never find peace; that settled feeling you get when you are exactly where you want to be, with exactly the people you want to be with, doing exactly what you are supposed to be doing and so on and so on.

Sylvia is one of those people who, since she was a little child, is what most people would call a dreamer. She needed to be. To take her from her not-so-good life and to transport her to a life of incredible possibilities. But then it became a habit, a way of being. She moved jobs, she changed lovers, she even moved countries, but nothing really helped. Every now and again the urge was so great that no amount of meditation, therapy, or pleas could help her find what she was looking for.

The only constant in Sylvia's life is that she will never be satisfied enough. There are too many lives that she could be leading. There are too many people she could be with, too many places that could be just the right place to be.

Sylvia knows in her heart that the disturbance that she feels this morning, will probably subside for a while and she will eventually be able to carry on. The love and support that she gets, make her commit to the life she has, but on days like this, she gets her notepad and writes about all the lives that she would be living if she wasn't living this one. A friend once said to her. " You have a thousand dreams in your head, but you don't realise them". She prefers to think she has a thousand different lives that she can experience, even if only in her dreams.

The not-so-great act

For every person stuck in a broken system
keeping them in poverty
For every broken heart looking for healing
For every broken family that can't even bear
staying in the same room with each other.
For every broken smile, accompanied, by teary
eyes, usually hidden behind fashionable shades.
For every broken parent filled with hopelessness
watching their children navigate through their
inner darkness.
For every broken person calling helplines after
hitting rock bottom.
For every single lost, hurt, and lonely feeling,
there is a perfectly crafted, flawless, beautiful
mask.

Bubbly

If my unsettled nature makes you
uncomfortable.
If my unpredictability scares you.
If my laughter is too loud, my gestures too
extravagant, let my bubbly self, get nearer, let
my warm touch reach your cold, bored soul until
fireworks brighten up the skies and I can politely
remind you, what fun really is.

Longing

Longing seems to be a constant in our lives. Longing to see someone that is no longer with us, longing to belong to a world that we increasingly feel detached from, longing to be loved without showing love for oneself, longing to belong to anything, a church, a book club, a family, another person (the most foolish of them all, as we are all alone after all). But longing doesn't get any harder or more unbearable than longing, without knowing what you are actually longing for.

Becoming invisible

When you get older at some stage you will become invisible. Heads won't turn when you enter a room, you will walk around pretty much unnoticed. Some people get quite upset about this, but I came to accept it as a fact of life.

Becoming invisible has its perks though. You can finally let go of the restraints of clothing, just in small ways mind you; not wearing bras or going back to wearing a bikini, that you were putting off wearing for years, even though your body spills out of it. By no means am I encouraging you to walk naked on the streets. It is against the law and, although you are invisible, it would still alarm some people. But you can get away with only wearing casual clothes whatever the time of the day and wherever you go, which is the second-best thing.

But the most important part of becoming invisible is that something happens inside of you; all the things you were too self-conscious about, suddenly become easy to do. So, you write a book, you travel alone, you say "no" more often (always politely, of course), and you stop caring so much about every little detail of your day. It's like life is slowly edging towards the end, so why waste time on things you don't really love or being with people you don't want to be around. Being invisible gives you the special power of self-preservation.

Misery loves company

When you are having a midlife crisis, remember to get away from predictable expectations. Don't buy a sports car, have an affair, shave your hair or buy an electric guitar, no, these are too simple, anyway, your difficulties can barely be considered a crisis. Instead, surround yourself with others that are having midlife crises too and go rock climbing, travel to places where you could be eaten by a saltwater crocodile, and do a parachute jump (actually, do this one, even if you are not going through a crisis). Get a book, and a warm drink, sit quietly, and ask yourself what was all that fuss about.

I'm the one who leaves

I'm not the one that is desperately clinging, begging to stay together.

I'm not the one that gets heartbroken and cries myself to sleep.

I'm not the one that, in a last attempt to stay together, blurts out "I can love enough for both of us!"

I'm the one who leaves.

I'm not the one that loses the ability to enjoy anything: from books to films, friends, or even life.

I'm not the one that experiences the excruciating pain of having someone fall out of love with them.

I'm not the one that will need to survive, despite the intense feelings of sorrow and sadness.

I'm the one that apologises for the pain I'm causing, with eyes wet from guilty tears, a heavy heart, and a packed suitcase.

I'm the one who leaves.

All about you

You are responsible for all my dreams and
nightmares
My lack of motivation and sleep
You are the pain in my right hip.

Doctors think I have all sorts of illnesses and
ailments
But I know it is you!
You that has no idea of the pain you caused.

You that make my heart ache and my body shake
Sometimes from the pain, sometimes from the
pleasure
From memories that still remain.

In my mind, I talk to you and ask you to leave,
Take with you every lasting feeling,
They should not be here.

In this one-way dialogue, you always smile and
say
I'm not here or there, I left you long ago,
It is you that need to let me go.

Summer in England

Nothing makes you feel more like an
Englishman than stripping your shirt off and
mowing the grass on a warm summer day!

People

I have met a great number of people in life,
some made me laugh, some made me cry, some
made me believe in destiny, and some made me
wonder what kind of cruel joke the universe was
playing on me, but none, and I mean not one
single one of them made me feel the way you
do. Now, that is something.

Potato soup

Wife: Dinner is ready! lovely, lumpy, potato soup just the way you like it.
Husband: No, I don't. I thought you liked lumpy potato soup.
Wife: No! I don't.
Husband: Why have you always made it lumpy then?"
Wife: Because I thought that is how you like it.
They looked at each in confusion that broke out into laughter, twenty years into marriage, and they just realised neither of them ever liked lumpy potato soup.

We are all broken

We are like a mosaic of pain, trauma, loss,
sadness, anger, unresolved,
unloved.
We keep getting broken and then putting
ourselves together again,
and again, we do it continuously throughout life
as it is the one way to heal and carry on.

Baker

If you have to choose a profession, become a baker, I cannot think of another profession where you relentlessly and repeatedly punch and hit something and turn it into one of the most delicious foods known to men.

Best day so far

I wish that every day for as long you live, at the
end of the day
You can say "this was my best day so far", and
every day be a little better,
A little brighter, a little more fun, you have a
little more laughter and love, and for
as long I live, I will be there, to watch over you.

Thoughts

Everywhere went silent, except my head, where
thoughts were dancing, twirling, jumping,
making so much noise, it was impossible to
sleep, so I did not fight, I did not resist, I just
stayed still and let them be.

Stay

Don't stay because is simpler to do so.
Don't stay because change is scary.
Don't stay because one's suffering is your
suffering too.
Don't stay because on a handful of days you
would not wish for anything but this life.
Stay if your soul smiles at the decision.
Stay if the love you feel is enough to overcome
the difficulties.
Stay if the rainy days are still seen as an excuse
for cuddling up on the sofa.
Stay if the alternatives don't make your heart
soar.
Stay if the idea of staying fills you with hope,
not despair.

Choose you

Every minute of every day, you have a choice to be you or to pretend to be someone others want you to be.

Every attitude, every answer, every interaction you are choosing between the two, choosing the latter makes you, little by little lose yourself.

In the beginning is a smile, when all you wanted was to cry, is saying everything is ok, when it isn't, is not answering the phone, because you know that your voice would falter, and you would have to come up with an excuse. Later it becomes a habit, you forget what you like and what you don't like, everything becomes, yes, that is fine. The answers are always very exciting and monosyllabic - Sure! Cool! Great! After all, the last thing you want is that anybody notices the real feelings behind the words.

So life goes on, and every time, you do or say something that goes against what you really want, a little piece of you just falls off, a little piece of you that was left on the sofa, when you said ok to watch a movie that you knew would make you have nightmares for weeks, another little piece stayed at the boat when you agreed to jump in the middle of the sea, knowing just how terrified you are of being in the water or when you accepted going for dinner with people that you really can't stand, the list is endless.

Every time that a little piece of you falls off and gets lost around, you change, your days become unbearably the same, all the routines you created yourself, now suffocate you, and all the little pieces you left along the way makes you feel so incomplete and lost, that slowly in this immense amount of losses you lose de ability to take a risk, to live impulsively, to find yourself.

A dark little corner

It was left there, abandoned, unwanted.
Yet it survived, despite the lack of light, and
hope, it persisted.
Like the roots of a tree trying to break through
concrete, it forced its way out again, after an
incredible effort, it finally saw a little light, and
its resolve became stronger,
It eventually saw the light brightened it up and it
found its way back, but now
It was not the same love it once was, it couldn't
possibly be, it changed, it had marks, grooves,
missing pieces, it had proof that it had been in a
not-so-good place, but above all, It proved its
resilience and determination.

Ingram Content Group UK Ltd.
Milton Keynes UK
UKHW021128180423
420361UK00015B/1126